MW01504310

A Sense of Life

A Sense of Life

Vol. I

KENNETH H. BAKER

Library of Congress Number:		2003093943
ISBN:	Hardcover	978-1-4134-1485-1
	Softcover	978-1-4134-1484-4

This book was printed in the United States of America.

To order additional copies of this book, contact:
Kenneth Baker
PO Box 1908
Orting, WA 98360

Contents

Introduction

A sense of life

A SENSE OF life is the sum total of a person's beliefs, values, morals and codes of conduct. It is the essence of a person's character and is an implicit part of every choice or value-judgement we make.

A sense of life is, at the core, a complex psychological mechanism which represents an integrated sum of our values. It serves as a standard to guide our behavior and an aid in decision making. It is formed over time by the events and interactions of our personal histories and contains elements from formal education and informal experiences both social and personal.

A sense of life may not always be a matter of conscious focus or the result of cognitive processes. It is frequently more subtle and implicit rather than logical and explicit. Though it may not reach the level of conscious awareness, our sense of life underlies and gives unity to our existence and serves as a basis for judging both ourselves and others. It is a source of reference to guide our actions both private and public.

It is unlikely that many of us could precisely define or explain our sense of life. We are frequently only vaguely aware of the system of beliefs and values that make up our sense of life. It is a constant factor of our daily existence, but we seldom devote time or energy to defining or stating our sense of life in a formal or systematic way.

The statements in this book are expressions of my personal sense of life and are intended to reflect life as I see it. All of the statements are original with me and have not been copied or quoted from any other source. I have made a conscious effort to eliminate inconsistencies or contradictions and have also made an effort to avoid redundancies.

happiness

those who
know the
real meaning
of genuine
happiness

realize that
being happy
depends upon
how you
feel about
your <u>self</u>

and not
upon how
others feel
about you

choices

regardless
of the
external circumstances

or internal
conditions

there are
always choices
we can make

we are never
without options

when it comes
to making decisions
about our lives

permission

we do not
need the
permission
of anyone

to experience
the essence
of
existence

no one
has to
grant us
the right
to be
fully alive

both ways

we can't
have it
both ways

we can't
have our
cake and
eat it too

all we
can do

is to
choose wisely

and accept
the consequences
of our choices

if only/what if

why do we
waste
our days

trapped between
if only
and
what if

if only
is regret
for the
past

what if
is fear
of the
future

creating

no building
we may
design
or construct

no work
of art
or poetry
or literature

can compare
with the
creation

of a healthy
and happy
<u>self</u>

locus of control

control is
a central factor
in our lives

if our behavior
is influenced
primarily by

what others
think
or say
or do

the locus
of control
is external

rather than
internal

friendship

genuine friendship
based upon
mutual trust

and a shared
sense of life

can give comfort
in times
of stress

support
in times of crisis

and feedback
in times
of doubt

eyes

our eyes
reveal more
about ourselves

than anything
we may say or do

we can mislead
with our words

and deceive
with our actions

but we
can never
lie with our eyes

signs

insensitivity
stems from
stupidity

cruelty
is an expression
of weakness

kindness
is a symbol
of maturity

gentleness
is a
sign of strength

winners

winners may not
set records
or capture trophies

they may not
make headlines
or experience success
in the marketplace

a real winner
is one who has
a strong sense
of personal identity

and has been able
to achieve
and maintain
genuine self-esteem

legacy

the regrets
we carry
within us

is the residue
of unresolved
conflicts and
unsettled debts

the unfinished business
of our
personal history

haunts our
memories
and diminishes

the enjoyment
we experience
in the present

silence

silence
is never
golden

when we
allow others
to violate
our rights
or destroy
our values

silence
is consent
if we permit
anyone to
victimize
the <u>self</u>

spirit

the human spirit
has a way
of surviving

the most painful
experiences

without losing

the will
to seek
and find
meaning
in existence

in love

it's the
easiest thing
in the world

to fall in love

it's the
hardest thing
in the world

to stay
in love

strength

strength is seldom
measured in
muscle power

the ability
to endure
pain and deprivation

with grace
and dignity

demonstrates
a stronger
character

and firmness
of spirit

than any feats
of brute force

giving up

we have all
known times
when we wanted

to simply
give up

giving up
is sometimes
easier
than fighting
the battle
any longer

the only time
giving up
is justified
is when

the only alternative
is to
give in

consensus

truth
is seldom
a matter
of consensus

the <u>self</u>
will never
learn
what is real

by believing
what the majority
knows
or thinks
or feels

character

character is a
rare quality
of a very
special kind

strength of character
is expressed by
the determination

to live life
to the fullest
regardless of

personal circumstances
or social conditions

needs/wants

the healthiest
people
are those
who can
distinguish

between
needs
and
wants

meeting needs
is essential

satisfying wants
may be nice
but not
necessary

means/ends

we each
have the choice

of living
our lives

as a means
to an end
for others

or to exist
as an end
for ourselves

allowing

allowing
our happiness
to be determined

by what
others think
or feel
or do

is to permit
those around us
to decide

the amount
of joy
we derive
from being alive

mixture

achieving
the proper
mixture

of personal goals
and
professional success

requires maintaining
a delicate balance

between
private integrity

and
public ambition

weakness

weakness
is most often
associated

with a lack of
physical strength

the most common
and the most
serious weaknesses

are those
which are revealed

by the lack
of personal
or social
or political
courage

security

security comes
not from
other people

or things
or places

but rather
from knowing
how to cope

with anything
life may bring

stability

achieving stability
is not
a matter

of being able
to maintain
a constant
external environment

but rather

the ability
to sustain
an inner equilibrium

in the face
of certain change

judgements

making judgements
is an
automatic function
of the
human mind

we cannot keep
from making judgements

the only
choice
we have
is whether
or not

to express
the judgements
we have made

directions

those decisions
which must
be made

in order
to change
the direction
of our lives

may involve
painful losses
and unknown
consequences

barriers

we sometimes
create barriers
where none exist

we build
walls between
ourselves
and others

to protect
the <u>self</u>
from being
exploited or abused

being cautious
is reasonable

being defensive
causes alienation

caring

caring
for those
who are
important
to you

can cause
harm
to the ones
you love

unless
you possess
a healthy
and honest
caring for
your <u>self</u>

stuck

there are times
in every life

when we
become stuck
in a place
a job
or a relationship

it may be
that only time
will release us

from the bondage
of the routine
and familiar

anger

anger need not
be considered
a negative emotion

honest anger
in response
to injustice
or discrimination
or mindless violence

is the sign
of a healthy
value system

looking back

looking back
for those who
are unhappy
in the present

is a painful
experience

remembering
for those
who are happy
in the
here and now

can be
a source
of genuine
pleasure

inhibitions

how often
do we allow
childish inhibitions

to rob us
of the pleasure
life has
to offer

being free
to enjoy
existence

does not mean
being irresponsible

selective

being selective
in the
things
we do

in the people
we choose
as friends

and in the
way we
spend our time

does not
necessarily represent
insecurity or conceit

it could express
a strong sense
of personal identity

differences

differences
can be real
or imaginary

they can be
significant
or unimportant

they can
create problems
or lead
to solutions

wherever
differences exist

we must deal
with them
or allow them
to control our lives

toughness

toughness
is the ability
to endure

any hardship
or deprivation

to persevere
in the face
of any obstacle

without becoming
hard or cynical
in the process

egoism / egotism

an emotional healthy
individual
is one who

values the <u>self</u>
above all other
<u>selves</u>

this is not
false pride or
infantile egotism

but genuine
love of <u>self</u>
expressed as
authentic self-esteem

private time

commitments
bind us
to a
public schedule

the pressure
builds a
heavy web

trapping us
in a busy world
of others

we need
some measure
of aloneness

we must have
private time

independence

we reveal
the level
of our
self-esteem

by the way
we respond
to events
in our lives

genuine self-esteem
is independent
of external events

authentic self-esteem
is never determined
by what others

may think
or feel
or do

denial

denial is the
most universal
psychological
defense mechanism

we protect our
emotional lives

by refusing
to admit that
reality is real

we hide
from life
because we
do not have

the courage
to deal
with the truth

doubt

doubting
when there
is good and
sufficient reason

may prevent
errors in judgement

and the negative
consequences
of poor decisions

skepticism
is healthy

unless it
is expressed
as a
bitter cynicism

individualism

an individualist
is not
a mindless
non-conformist

or a rebel
without a cause

an authentic
individualist
is a person

with a strong
sense of
personal identity

and the courage
to live life
on his
own terms

time outs

each of us
needs to take
an occasional
time out

we need
to step back
from the general
business of living

to assess
where we've been

and where
we're going

pause for just
a moment
to get in touch
with the <u>self</u>

knowing when

knowing when
a change
is necessary

and having
the courage
to let go
of the known

to reach out
for something
new and different

requires courage
and a strong
sense of <u>self</u>

privacy

the right
to privacy

is not just
a social concession

or political
compromise

it is an
absolute essential

to any society
which claims

to honor
the individual